Welcome Back to Mu

Let's review our notes and bow hold.

Be sure to follow your teacher's directions.

Open String Review

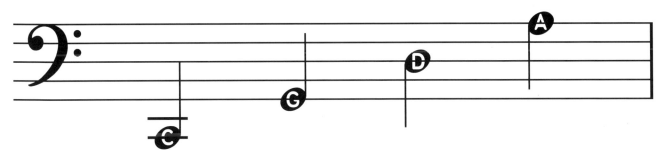

The Bow Hold

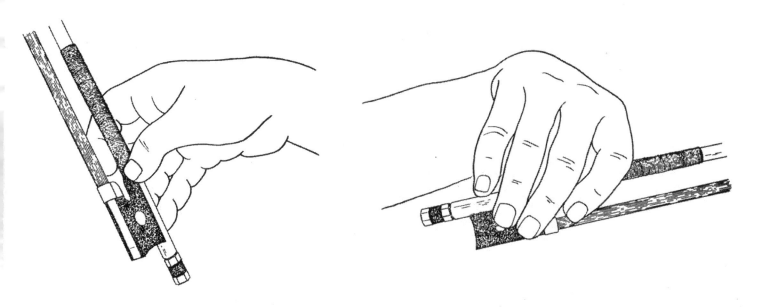

2 Note Review

First finger on "D"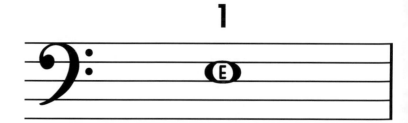

First, second and third fingers on "D"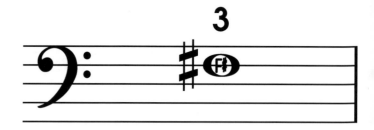

Four fingers on "D"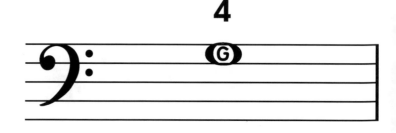

First finger on "A"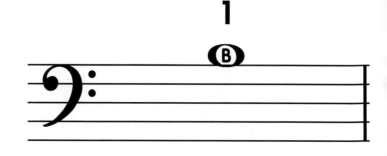

Au Claire de la Lune

Hot Cross Buns

Good King Wenceslas

Mary Had a Little Lamb

Lightly Row

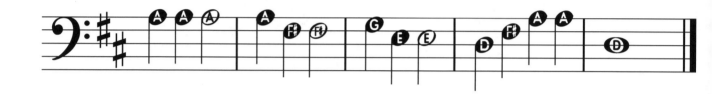

Aura Lee

Go Tell Aunt Rhody

Frog Song

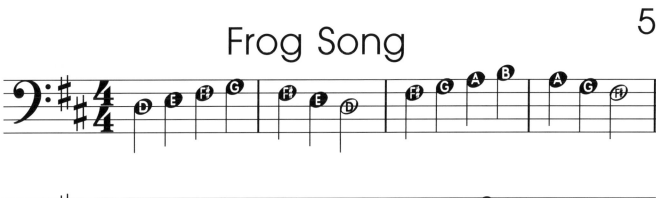

Camptown Races

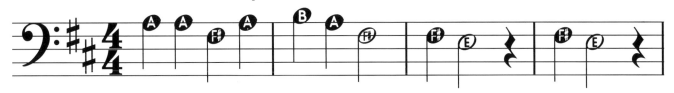

London Bridge

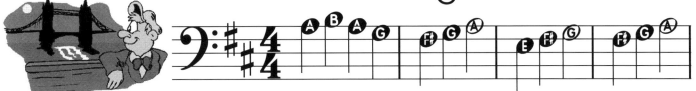
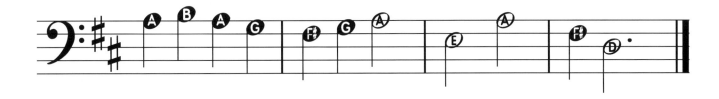

Dreydl, Dreydl

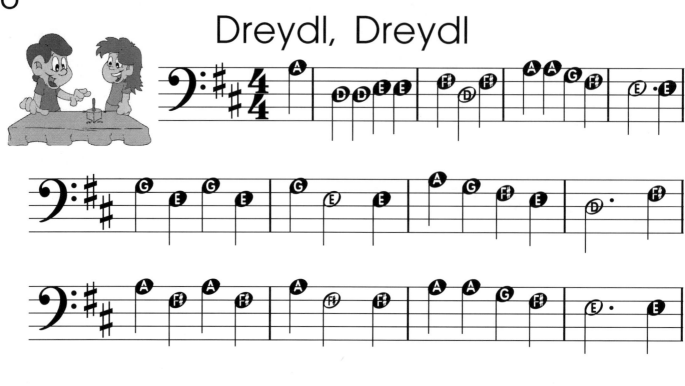

Twinkle, Twinkle, Little Star

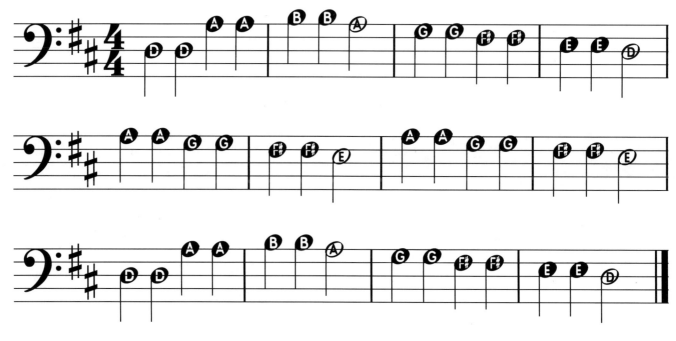

Jolly Old St. Nicholas

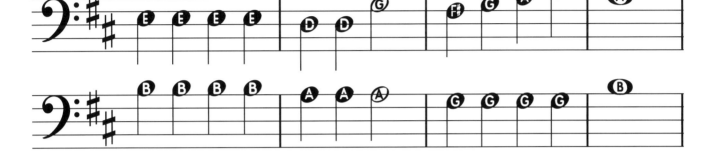

The Bridge at Avignon

Are You Sleeping?

Musette

10
Lo Yisa Goy

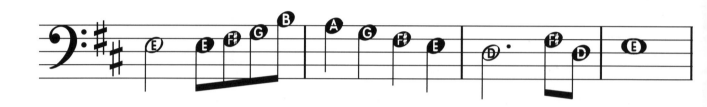
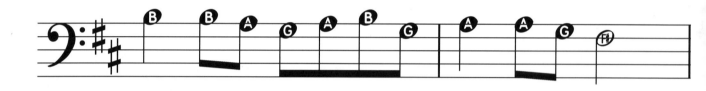
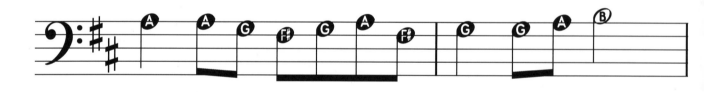
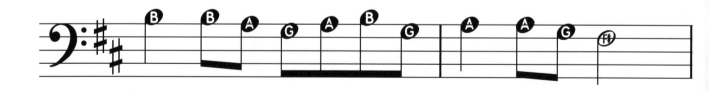
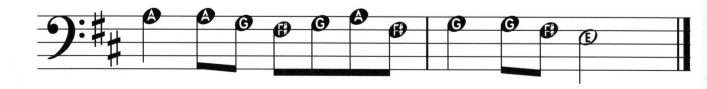

Baa Baa Black Sheep

Symphony No.1 by Brahms

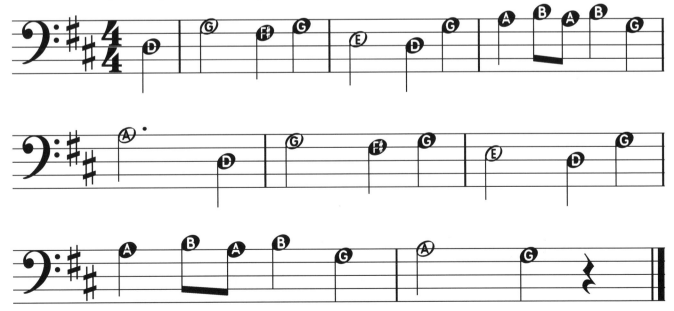

12 This Little Light of Mine

Up on the House Top

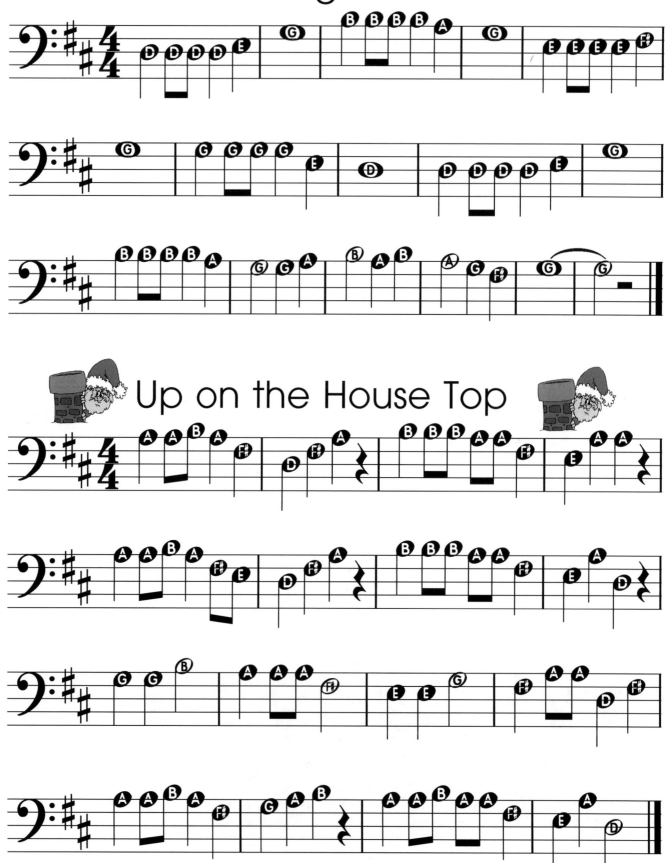

This Old Man

Old MacDonald

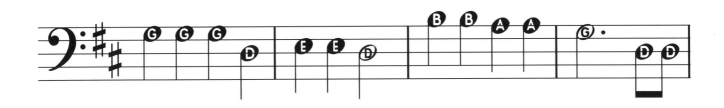

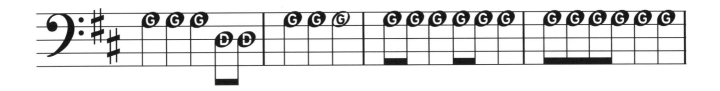

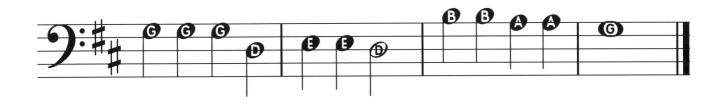

14 Spring Theme from the Four Seasons

Rock-a-my-Soul

15

Largo from New World Symphony

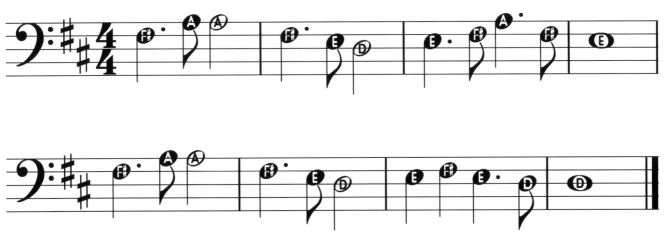

Kum Ba Yah

Ode to Joy

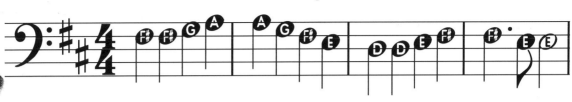
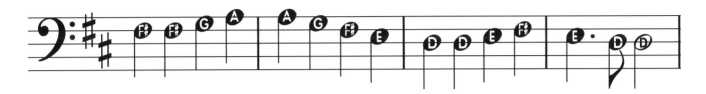
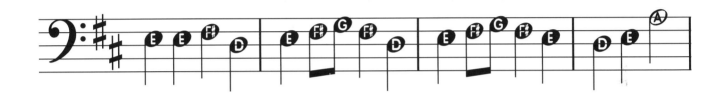
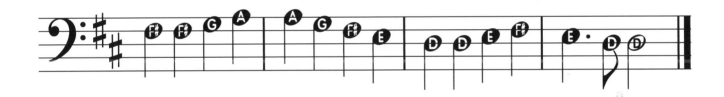

Oh, Susana

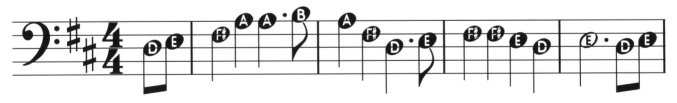

Shepherd's Hey

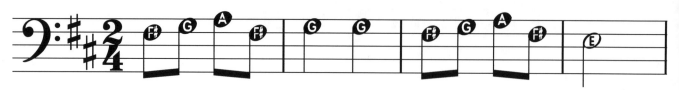
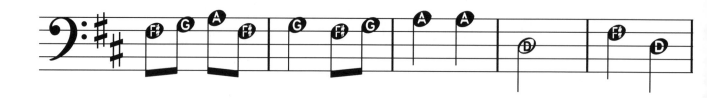
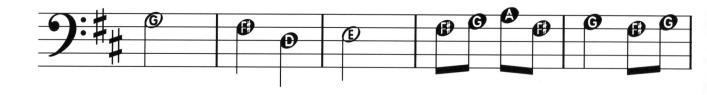

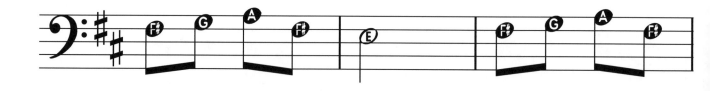
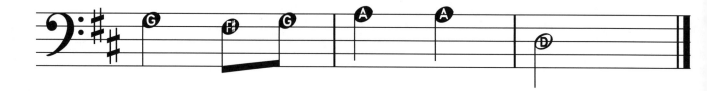

More Note Review and Exercises

19

Three fingers on "A" **C SHARP**

C SHARP on the "A" String

Four fingers on "A" **HIGH D**

HIGH D on the "A" String

22 The next several pages are for violins learning the "E" string. This cello music allows you to play along while they learn some new notes on their "E" string.

"E" on the D

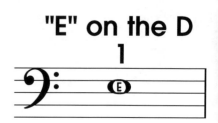

1.

2.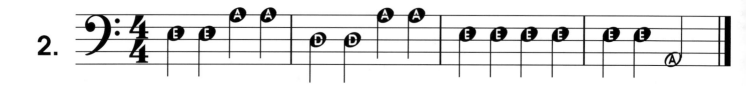

"F" SHARP

Three fingers on D

3.

4.

5.

1.

2.

3.

4.

5.

1.

2.

3.

This is a harmony part to be played with the violins.

Mary Had A Little Lamb

1.
2.
3.
4.
5.

27

1.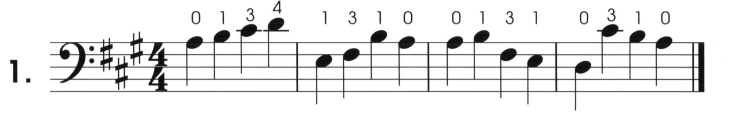

2.

3.

4.

28

1.

2.

3.

4.

5.

Songs in the Key of "E"

29

Lightly Row

Aura Lee

Go Tell Aunt Rhody

Four by Four

4th Finger Marathon

This Old Man

OPEN "G" STRING
NEW NOTE — OPEN

"Low A" on G string
NEW NOTE — First finger on G string — 1

1.
2.
3.

4.

"LOW B" on G string

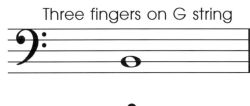

33

1.

2.

3.

4.

5.

34

1.

2.

3.

Mary Had A Little Lamb

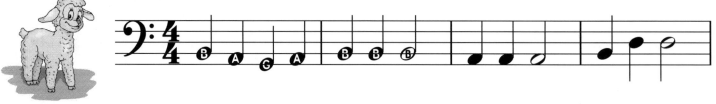

"C" on the "G" string

Four fingers on G string

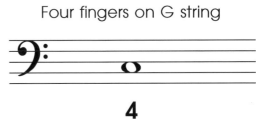

35

1.

2.

3.

4.

5.

Fingers on the "G" String

Scotland's Burning

G Major Scale

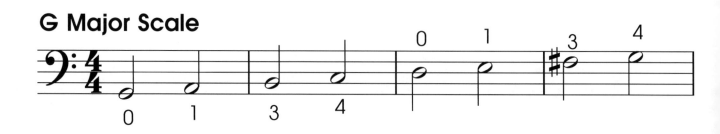

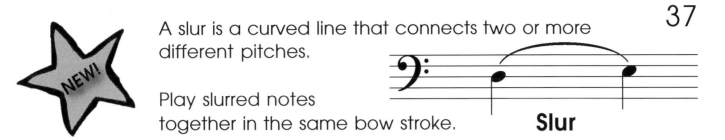

"F" Natural
2nd Finger

Playing "F" Natural

Hot Cross Buns

The Snake Charmer

"C" Natural
Two Fingers on A

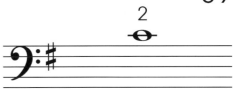

Two fingers on "A" string

Playing "C" Natural

Hot Cross Buns

Snake Charmer

40

Half Step Song on "D"

Half Step Song on "A"

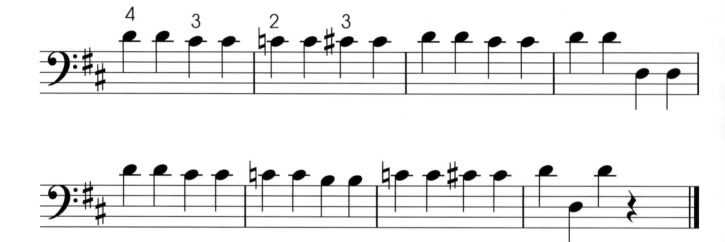

C Major Scale

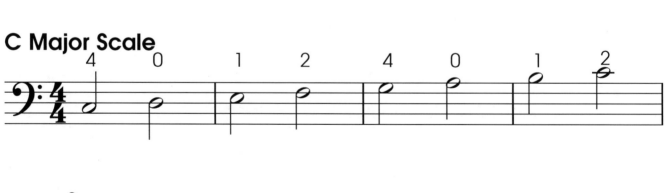

Sakura

42

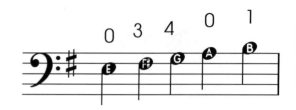

Low 2 on E March

Fun on the (Violin)E String

G Major Scale
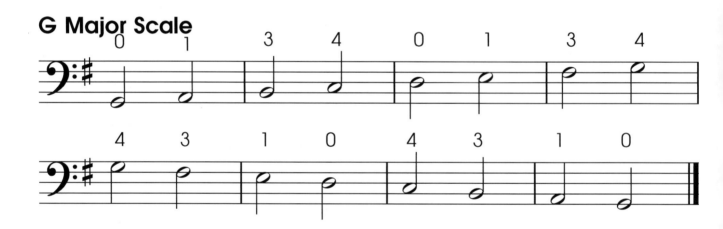

Finale from the "New World Symphony"

Simple Gifts

Rhythm Fun

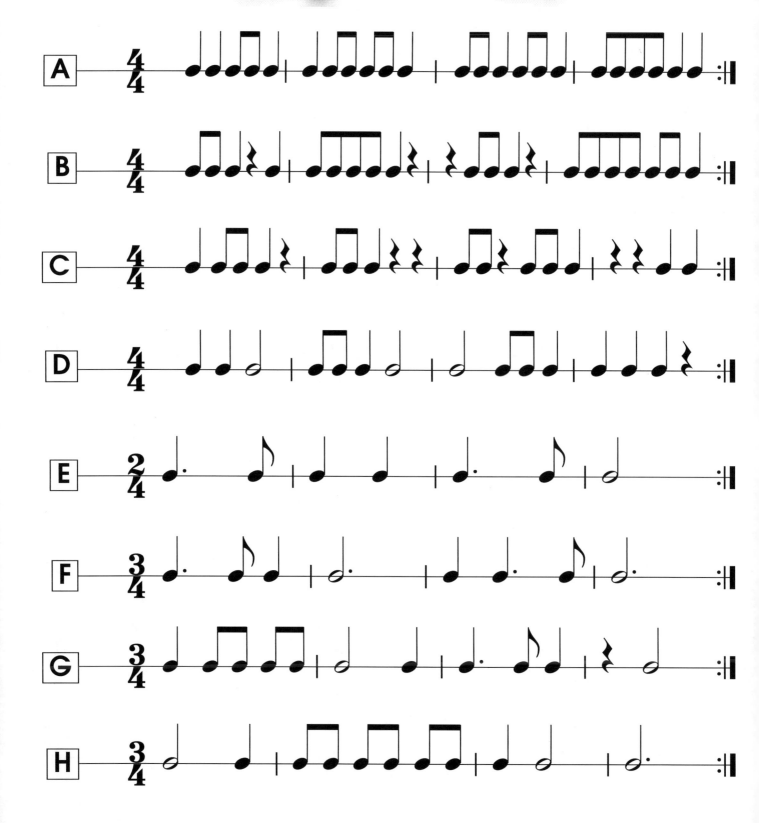

Made in the USA
Las Vegas, NV
11 July 2023

74521328R00026